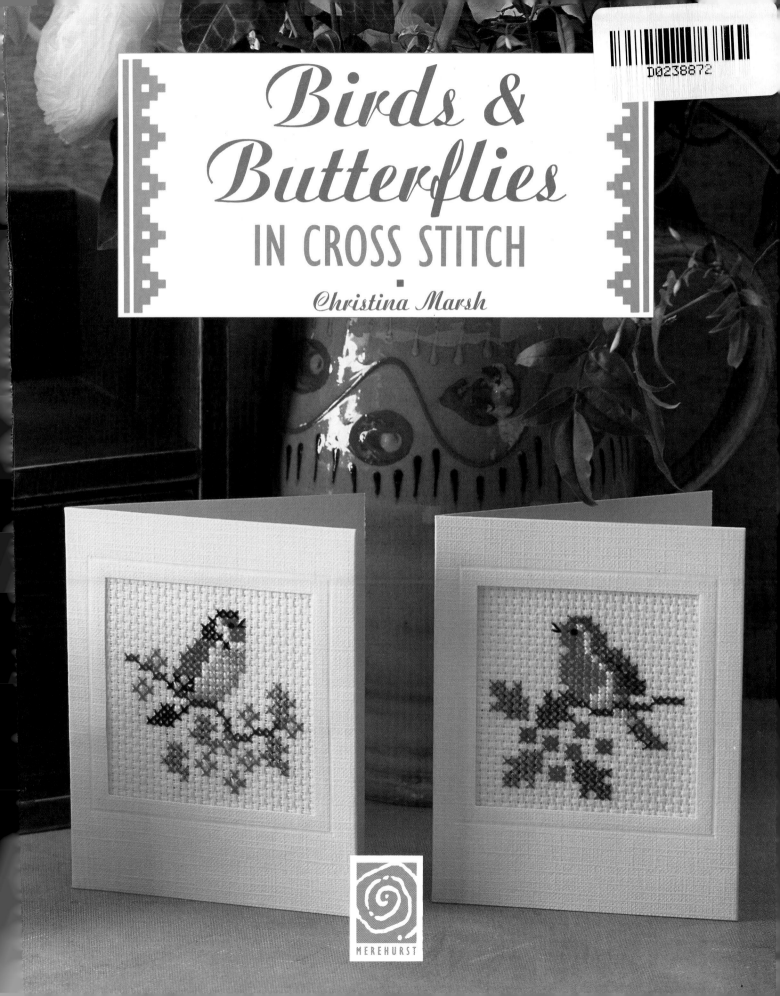

Birds & Butterflies
IN CROSS STITCH

Christina Marsh

MEREHURST

THE CHARTS

Some of the designs in this book are very detailed and due to inevitable space limitations, the charts may be shown on a comparatively small scale; in such cases, readers may find it helpful to have the particular chart with which they are currently working enlarged.

THREADS

The projects in this book were all stitched with Anchor stranded cotton embroidery threads. The keys given with each chart also list thread combinations for those who wish to use DMC or Madeira threads.
It should be pointed out that the shades produced by different companies vary slightly, and it is not always possible to find identical colours in a different range.

First published in 1996 by Merehurst Limited
Ferry House, 51-57 Lacy Road, Putney, London SW15 1PR
Text, photography & illustrations © Copyright 1996 Merehurst Limited
ISBN 1 85391 458 4

A catalogue record for this book is available from the British Library.

Edited by Diana Lodge
Designed by Maggie Aldred
Photography by Marie-Louise Avery
Illustrations by John Hutchinson (pp5-7) and King & King (pp7 and 31)
Typesetting by Dacorum Type & Print, Hemel Hempstead
Colour separation by Fotographics Limited, UK – Hong Kong
Printed in Hong Kong by Wing King Tong

Merehurst is the leading publisher of craft books and has an excellent range of titles to suit all levels. Please send to the address above for our free catalogue, stating the title of this book.

CONTENTS

INTRODUCTION

Birds and butterflies are an endless source of inspiration for me, in both my painting and my embroidery. With so many birds to chose from, I was spoilt for choice when creating the designs in this collection. However, I hope there is something for everyone; ranging from small garden birds to exotic birds of the rain forests. It was equally difficult choosing the butterflies, but again I hope you enjoy stitching the wide variety of designs, from the unashamed beauty of the Peacock to the lacy delicacy of the Marbled White.

Many of the projects in this book have been designed for the beginner or for those with limited time for sewing, but there are a number of more ambitious projects, such as the Tropical Birds cushion, intended for the experienced embroiderer. All the projects are worked on easy-to-sew Aida fabric; if you prefer to work on linen, however, you can simply substitute 28-count linen for those designs stitched on 14-count Aida. In order to reduce the amount of time required for each project, I have also avoided the use of three-quarter stitches.

These designs can be used in a variety of ways; for example, the bird portraits featured on the greetings cards could be displayed as a set of miniatures, while the butterfly designs shown on coasters would look equally delightful on scented sachets.

Birds and butterflies are such enchanting creatures that it was a joy to create the projects contained in this book, and I hope that you will experience equal pleasure in stitching them.

BASIC SKILLS

∎

BEFORE YOU BEGIN

PREPARING THE FABRIC
Even with an average amount of handling, many evenweave fabrics tend to fray at the edges, so it is a good idea to overcast the raw edges, using ordinary sewing thread, before you begin.

FABRIC
The projects in this book use Aida fabric, which is ideal both for beginners and more advanced stitchers as it has a surface of clearly designated squares. All Aida fabric has a count, which refers to the number of squares (each stitch covers one square) to one inch (2.5cm); the higher the count, the smaller the finished stitching. Projects in this book use 11- and 14-count Aida, popular and readily available sizes, in a wide variety of colours.

THE INSTRUCTIONS
Each project begins with a full list of the materials that you will require. The measurements given for the embroidery fabric include a minimum of 5cm (2in) all around to allow for stretching it in a frame and preparing the edges to prevent them from fraying.

Colour keys for stranded embroidery cottons – Anchor, DMC or Madeira – are given with each chart. It is assumed that you will need to buy one skein of each colour mentioned in a particular key, even though you may use less, but where two or more skeins are needed, this information is included in the main list of requirements.

Before you begin to embroider, always mark the centre of the design with two lines of basting stitches, one vertical and one horizontal, running from edge to edge of the fabric, as indicated by the arrows on the charts.

As you stitch, use the centre lines given on the chart and the basting threads on your fabric as reference points for counting the squares and threads to position your design accurately.

WORKING IN A HOOP

A hoop is the most popular frame for use with small areas of embroidery. It consists of two rings, one fitted inside the other; the outer ring usually has an adjustable screw attachment so that it can be tightened to hold the stretched fabric in place. Hoops are available in several sizes, ranging from 10cm (4in) in diameter to quilting hoops with a diameter of 38cm (15in). Hoops with table stands or floor stands attached are also available.

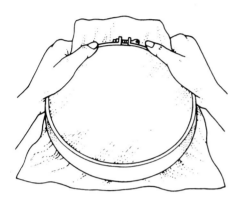

1 To stretch your fabric in a hoop, place the area to be embroidered over the inner ring and press the outer ring over it, with the tension screw released. Tissue paper can be placed between the outer ring and the embroidery, so that the hoop does not mark the fabric. Lay the tissue paper over the fabric when you set it in the hoop, then tear away the central embroidery area.

2 Smooth the fabric and, if necessary, straighten the grain before tightening the screw. The fabric should be evenly stretched.

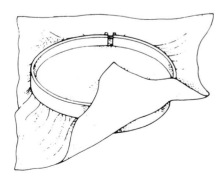

WORKING IN A RECTANGULAR FRAME

Rectangular frames are more suitable for larger pieces of embroidery. They consist of two rollers, with tapes attached; and two flat side pieces, which slot into the rollers and are held in place by pegs or screw attachments. Available in different sizes, either alone or with adjustable table or floor stands, frames are measured by the length of the roller tape, and range in size from 30cm (12in) to 68cm (27in).

As alternatives to a slate frame, canvas stretchers and the backs of old picture frames can be used. Provided there is sufficient extra fabric around the finished size of the embroidery, the edges can be turned under and simply attached with drawing pins (thumb tacks) or staples.

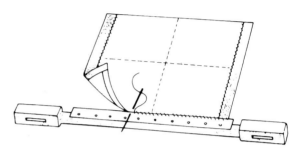

1 To stretch your fabric in a rectangular frame, cut out the fabric, allowing at least an extra 5cm (2in) all around the finished size of the embroidery. Baste a single 12mm (½in) turning on the top and bottom edges and oversew strong tape, 2.5cm (1in) wide, to the other two sides. Mark the centre line both ways with basting stitches. Working from the centre outward and using strong thread, oversew the top and bottom edges to the roller tapes. Fit the side pieces into the slots, and roll any extra fabric on one roller until the fabric is taut.

2 Insert the pegs or adjust the screw attachments to secure the frame. Thread a large-eyed needle (chenille needle) with strong thread or fine string and lace both edges, securing the ends around the intersections of the frame. Lace the webbing at 2.5cm (1in) intervals, stretching the fabric evenly.

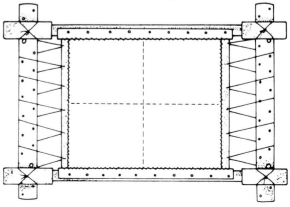

EXTENDING EMBROIDERY FABRIC

It is easy to extend a piece of embroidery fabric, such as a bookmark, to stretch it in a hoop.

● Fabric oddments of a similar weight can be used. Simply cut four pieces to size (in other words, to the measurement that will fit both the embroidery fabric and your hoop) and baste them to each side of the embroidery fabric before stretching it in the hoop in the usual way.

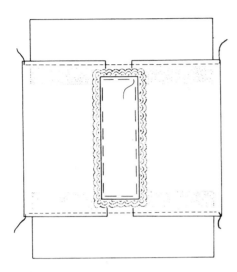

THE STITCHES

CROSS STITCH

For all cross stitch embroidery, the following two methods of working are used. In each case, neat rows of vertical stitches are produced on the back of the fabric.

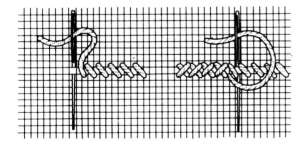

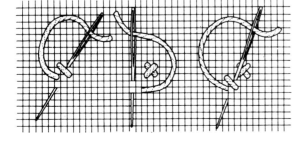

● When stitching large areas, work in horizontal rows. Working from right to left, complete the first row of evenly spaced diagonal stitches over the number of threads specified in the project instructions. Then, working from left to right, repeat the process. Continue in this way, making sure each stitch crosses in the same direction.

● When stitching diagonal lines, work downwards, completing each stitch before moving to the next. When starting a project always begin to embroider at the centre of the design and work outwards to ensure that the design will be placed centrally on the fabric.

BACKSTITCH

Backstitch is used in the projects to give emphasis to a particular foldline, an outline or a shadow. The stitches are worked over the same number of threads as the cross stitch, forming continuous straight or diagonal lines.

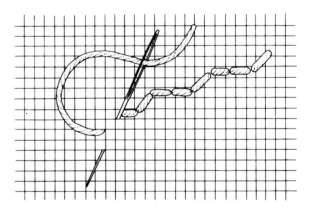

● Make the first stitch from left to right; pass the needle behind the fabric and bring it out one stitch length ahead to the left. Repeat and continue in this way along the line.

BUTTONHOLE STITCH

This is used to cover the rings attached to the jewellery boxes on page 12, the stitches being placed very close together to form a firm, well-covered edge. Holding the ring and the tail of thread in one hand, take the needle straight down behind the ring and bring the point out over the looped thread, as shown; make the next stitch as close to the previous stitch as possible, continuing until the entire ring is covered, with the edging on the outside. Cover the initial tail of thread with the final stitches, then take the needle through a few stitches to fasten off.

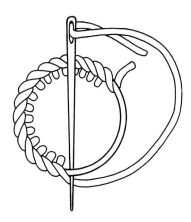

FRENCH KNOTS

This stitch is shown on some of the diagrams by a small dot. To work a french knot, bring your needle and cotton out slightly to the right of where you want your knot to be. Wind the thread once or twice around the needle, depending on how big you want your knot to be, and insert the needle to the left of the point where you brought it out.

Be careful not to pull too hard or the knot will disappear though the fabric. The instructions state the number of strands of cotton to be used for the french knots.

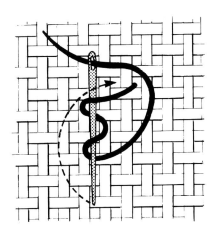

FINISHING

MOUNTING EMBROIDERY

The cardboard should be cut to the size of the finished embroidery, with an extra amount added all round to allow for the recess in the frame.

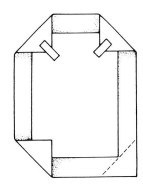 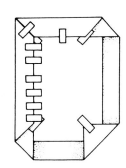

1 Place embroidery face down, with the cardboard centred on top, and basting and pencil lines matching. Begin by folding over the fabric at each corner and securing it with masking tape.

2 Working first on one side and then the other, fold over the fabric on all sides and secure it firmly with pieces of masking tape, placed about 2.5cm (1in) apart. Also neaten the mitred corners with masking tape, pulling the fabric tightly to give a firm, smooth finish.

HEAVIER FABRICS

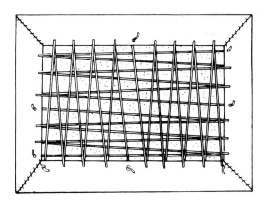

● Lay the embroidery face down, with the cardboard centred on top; fold over the edges of the fabric on opposite sides, making mitred folds at the corners, and lace across, using strong thread. Repeat on the other two sides. Finally, pull up the fabric firmly over the cardboard. Overstitch the mitred corners.

Through the Cherry Tree

Blue tits peep from the branches
of a fruiting cherry tree at an
idyllic country cottage. Blue tits
are frequent visitors to garden food
boxes, and both sexes have the same
familiar blue, green, yellow, black
and white colouring.

THROUGH THE CHERRY TREE

YOU WILL NEED

For the picture, set in a frame with an internal measurement of 30cm × 24.5cm (11½in × 9½in):

46cm × 38cm (18in × 15in) of cream,
11-count Aida fabric
Stranded embroidery cotton in the colours given in the panel
No24 tapestry needle
Picture frame as specified above
Firm card, to fit the frame
Lightweight synthetic batting/wadding,
the same size as the card
Strong thread for mounting
Paper glue stick

•

THE EMBROIDERY

Prepare the fabric as described on page 4; find the centre either by folding the fabric in half and then in half again, and lightly pressing the folded corner, or by marking the horizontal and vertical centre lines with basting stitches in a light-coloured thread. Mount the fabric in a frame (see page 5) and start the design from the centre.

Following the chart, complete all the cross stitching first, using two strands of thread in the needle. Finish with the backstitching, again using two strands of thread. Be careful not to take dark threads across the back of the work in such a way that they show through on the right side.

The brids' eyes, indicated by black dots on the chart, can either be made with a single french knot, stitched with two strands of black thread, or you can use a small black bead for each eye.

MOUNTING AND FRAMING

Remove the finished embroidery from the frame and wash if necessary, then press lightly on the wrong side, using a steam iron. Take extra care when pressing if you have used beads for the eyes. Spread glue evenly on one side of the mounting card, and lightly press the batting to the surface. Lace the embroidery over the padded surface (see page 7). Remove basting stitches; place the mounted embroidery in the frame, and assemble the frame according to the manufacturer's instructions.

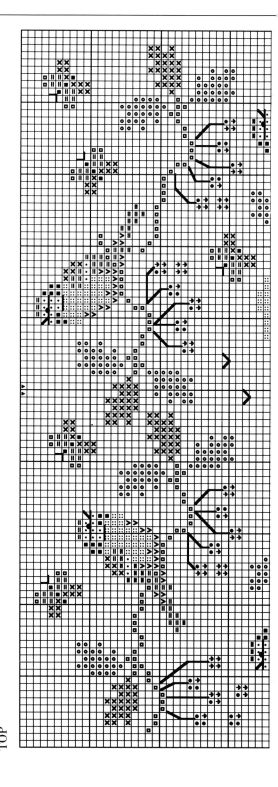

TOP

THROUGH THE CHERRY TREE ▲		ANCHOR	DMC	MADEIRA
•	White	1	White	White
■	Black	403	Black	Black
=	Blue	979	312	1005
::	Light yellow green	278	472	1414
V	Medium yellow green	280	733	1609

BOTTOM

		ANCHOR	DMC	MADEIRA
X	Medium green	267	580	1608
O	Dark green	268	935	1504
□	Dark brown	360	898	2006
●	Bright red	19	817	0212
↓	Deep red	20	498	0513

Note: backstitch cherry stems in dark green; blue tits' heads and beaks, birds in the sky and butterflies' antennae in black, and window outlines in medium yellow green; either use beads or french knots in two strands of black for blue tits' eyes.

Jewellery Boxes

Handmade jewellery or trinket boxes, the lids decorated with tiny butterfly motifs, make lovely gifts for special birthdays. If you wish to make an oblong box, use the same basic method and simply add more motifs to the top and bottom borders.

JEWELLERY BOXES

For the small box, 5cm (2in) deep, with a top
measuring 11.5cm (4½ in) square:

20cm (8in) square of rose, 14-count Aida fabric
Stranded embroidery cotton in the colours given in
the panel
No26 tapestry needle
Seven pieces of cotton fabric, each 14cm (5½in)
square
Stiff card (medium thickness) – four pieces 5cm ×
11.5cm (2in × 4½in), and four pieces 11.5cm (4½in)
square
Lightweight polyester batting/wadding – four pieces
5cm × 11.5cm (2in × 4½in), and one piece 11.5cm
(4½in) square
25cm (10in) of thin white cord
Small curtain ring
Glue stick
Masking tape
Strong thread for lacing

For the large box, 7.5cm (3in) deep, with a top
measuring 15cm (6in) square:

23cm (9in) square of rose, 14-count Aida fabric
Stranded embroidery cotton in the colours given in
the panel
No26 tapestry needle
Seven pieces of cotton fabric, each 19cm (7½in)
square
Stiff card (medium thickness) – four pieces 7.5cm ×
15cm (3in × 6in), and four pieces 15cm (6in) square
Lightweight polyester batting/wadding – four pieces
7.5cm × 15cm (3in × 6in), and one piece 15cm (6in)
square
33cm (13in) of thin white cord
Small curtain ring
Glue stick
Masking tape
Strong thread for lacing

●

THE EMBROIDERY

For each box, prepare the fabric as described on
page 4; find the centre either by folding the fabric in
half and then in half again, and lightly pressing the
folded corner, or by marking the horizontal and
vertical centre lines with basting stitches in a light-

coloured thread. Mount the fabric in a hoop or frame
(see pages 4-5) and start the design from the centre.

Following the chart, complete all the cross
stitching first, using two strands of thread in the
needle. Finish with the backstitching, again using
two strands of thread. Remove the finished
embroidery from the hoop or frame and wash if
necessary, then press lightly on the wrong side,
using a steam iron.

SMALL BOX

To prepare the side sections, first glue a piece of
batting to one side of each of the four 5cm ×
11.5cm (2in × 4½in) pieces of card. For each side,
take a piece of cotton fabric and lay a card, padded
side down, on the wrong side of the fabric, with an
allowance of 12mm (½in) of fabric showing at each
side, and 20mm (¾in) showing at the bottom edge.
Fold in the sides and tape them; bring the upper
section of the fabric over the card and, turning the
raw edge under by a generous 20mm (¾in), stitch
along the lower edge, so that the stitching line is just
slightly to the back of the card (not along the
bottom). Oversewing the edges with neat stitches,
join the four sides of the box together to make a
square, with the stitched lower edges facing inward.

Take the three square sections (base and inside
lid) and cover one side of each with a piece of fabric:
mitre the corners and fold in the sides, holding them
with tape (see page 7). With the fabric outside,
gently push one section into the base of the box and
neatly oversew the bottom edge on all sides. Turn the
box over and neatly stitch white cord along the top
edge of one side (now the back edge), allowing the
ends to run down the inside corners and on to the
base. Push the second base piece, fabric side up,
into the box, covering the cord ends and the back of
the first base section.

Glue batting to one side of the remaining
uncovered card, and lace the embroidery over this
side (see page 7). Place the two lid sections with
wrong sides together and neatly oversew the edges.
Stitch the lid to the cord at the back of the box.
Finally, buttonhole stitch over the curtain ring, using
six strands of thread in the needle (see page 6), and
stitch it to the front centre edge of the lid.

LARGE BOX

Follow the instructions given for the smaller box,
using the 7.5cm × 15cm (3in × 6in) card for the
sides and the 15cm (6in) square cards for the top
and base of the box.

JEWELLERY BOXES	ANCHOR	DMC	MADEIRA
□ White	1	White	White
○ Red	47	304	0510
■ Green	189	991	1204

Note: form each butterfly antenna with one straight stitch in red.

Tropical Birds Cushion

Inset in colourful fabric, this lively study of parrots will cheer up even the dullest winter's day. If you prefer, you could use a pale blue, green or yellow background.

TROPICAL BIRDS CUSHION

YOU WILL NEED

For the *Tropical Birds* cushion cover, measuring 53cm (21in) square:

*66cm (26in) of white, 11-count Aida fabric
Cotton fabric for cushion cover: one piece 54.5cm (21½in) square (for the back); two strips measuring 54.5cm × 7.5cm (21½in × 3in), and two 42cm × 7.5cm (16½in × 3in)
Stranded embroidery cotton in the colours given in the appropriate panel
No24 tapesty needle
Sewing cotton to match the fabric
Cushion pad 56cm (22in) square, for a well-padded effect*

•

THE EMBROIDERY

Prepare the fabric as described on page 4; find the centre by folding the fabric in half and then in half again, and lightly pressing the folded corner, or by marking the horizontal and vertical centre lines with basting stitches in a light-coloured thread. Mount the fabric in a frame (see page 5) and start the design from the centre.

Follow the chart, using three strands of thread in the needle throughout. Remove the finished embroidery from the frame; wash if necessary, then press lightly on the wrong side with a steam iron.

MAKING THE COVER

Keeping the embroidery centred, trim the fabric to a 42cm (16½in) square. With right sides together, and taking a 6mm (¼in) in seam allowance, machine stitch a short fabric strip to each side of the embroidery. Press seam allowances away from the embroidery. Join the two longer strips to the top and bottom of the work, and again press.

Place the embroidered front and back covers with right sides together and, again taking 6mm (¼in) seam allowances, machine around the edge, leaving a 46cm (18in) gap at one side edge. Trim away surplus fabric at corners to make turning easier; you may also wish to overlock raw edges to prevent fraying. Turn the cover right side out and insert the cushion pad. Fold in the remaining seam allowances, and slipstitch the opening.

TROPICAL BIRDS ▶	ANCHOR	DMC	MADEIRA
· White	1	White	White
H Black	403	Black	Black
− Yellow	305	743	0113
I Beige	831	3782	1907
o Light brown	371	433	2303
V Dark brown	360	898	2005
∶ Medium grey	399	318	1802
= Light turquoise	433	996	1103
□ Dark turquoise	410	995	1102
■ Navy	164	824	1006
◇ Bright red	334	606	0209
⊓ Medium red	46	666	0210
Ǝ Dark red	47	321	0511
T Light green	256	906	1411
⊠ Medium green	258	904	1413

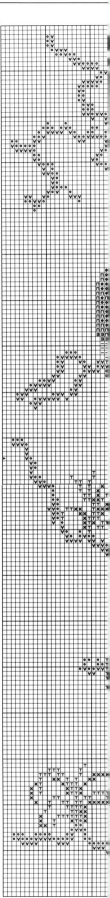

Butterfly Coasters

This charming and unusual set of coasters portrays five much-loved butterflies, frequently seen on waste land and along hedgerows. Two – the tortoiseshell and the painted lady – are often confused, but once stitched, never forgotten!

BUTTERFLY COASTERS

YOU WILL NEED

For each coaster, measuring 9cm (3½in) in diameter:

12.5cm (5in) square of 14-count Aida (fabric colours chosen for the coasters were antique white/tortoiseshell, cream/painted lady, rose/purple emperor, mid-blue/marbled white and light blue/peacock)
12.5cm (5in) square of iron-on interfacing
Stranded embroidery cotton in the colours given in the appropriate panel
No26 tapestry needle
Coaster, 9cm (3½in) in diameter (for suppliers, see page 40)

NOTE: one skein of each colour on the combined list is sufficient for all five designs

•

THE EMBROIDERY

Prepare the fabric as described on page 4; find the centre by folding the fabric in half and then in half again, and lightly pressing the folded corner, or by marking the horizontal and vertical centre lines with basting stitches in a light-coloured thread. If you are stitching several designs at once, allow an area 12.5cm (5in) square for each; separate design areas with lines of basting stitches, and mark the centre of each area, but do not cut them apart until you have finished the embroidery.

Mount the prepared fabric in a hoop or frame (see pages 4-5). Following the chart, complete all cross stitching, using two strands of thread in the needle. Finish with the backstitching, again using two strands of thread. Each antenna is embroidered with one long straight stitch.

FINISHING

Take the finished embroidery from the frame and remove any basting stitches. Wash if necessary, then press lightly on the wrong side, using a steam iron. If you are making several coasters, cut them apart along the basted dividing lines. For each coaster, lay the interfacing with its adhesive side down on the wrong side of the embroidery and press lightly.

Lay the embroidery right side up and place the transparent backing of the coaster over it. Taking care to ensure that the embroidery is centred, mark around the backing disc with a pencil. Using this line as a cutting guide, carefully trim away surplus fabric (the interfacing will help to prevent fraying). Place the butterfly in the coaster and secure it, following the manufacturer's instructions.

BUTTERFLY COASTERS (all five)	ANCHOR	DMC	MADEIRA
• White	1	White	White
■ Black	403	Black	Black
□ Dark brown	905	3031	2003
‖ Dark warm brown	381	938	2006
T Warm brown	360	898	2005
V Light brown	375	420	2104
∣ Rust	339	920	0401
↓ Deep rust	340	919	0314
+ Deep red	20	814	0513
X Deep orange	316	740	0204
∙∙ Light orange	314	741	0201
− Yellow	891	676	2208
= Mauve	118	3746	0902
∷ Light blue	145	799	0911
O Medium blue	148	311	0912
⦿ Dark blue	149	823	0913

MARBLED WHITE ▼	ANCHOR	DMC	MADEIRA
• White	1	White	White
■ Black	403	Black	Black
‖ Dark warm brown	381	938	2006
T Warm brown	360	898	2005
V Light brown	375	420	2104

Note: backstitch lines on wings in warm brown; each antenna is made with one black straight stitch.

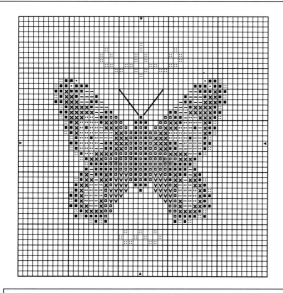

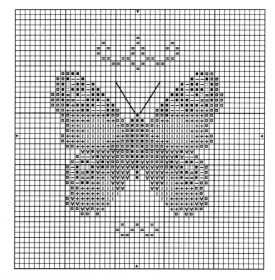

TORTOISESHELL ▲		ANCHOR	DMC	MADEIRA
·	White	1	White	White
■	Black	403	Black	Black
□	Dark brown	905	3031	2003
V	Light brown	375	420	2104
X	Deep orange	316	740	0204
⋅⋅	Light orange	314	741	0201
—	Yellow	891	676	2208
∷	Light blue	145	799	0911

Note: each antenna is made with one black straight stitch.

PEACOCK ▲		ANCHOR	DMC	MADEIRA
■	Black	403	Black	Black
□	Dark brown	905	3031	2003
V	Light brown	375	420	2104
I	Rust	339	920	0401
+	Deep red	20	814	0513
=	Mauve	118	3746	0902
∷	Light blue	145	799	0911
—	Yellow	891	676	2208

Note: backstitch lines on wings in black; each antenna is made with one black straight stitch.

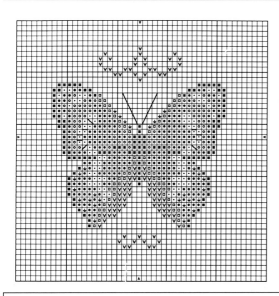

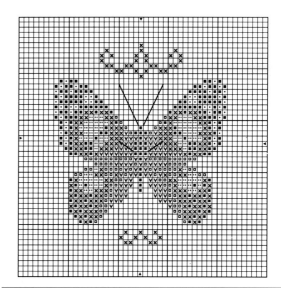

PURPLE EMPEROR ▲		ANCHOR	DMC	MADEIRA
·	White	1	White	White
■	Black	403	Black	Black
□	Dark brown	905	3031	2003
V	Light brown	375	420	2104
↓	Deep rust	340	919	0314
●	Dark blue	149	823	0913
○	Medium blue	148	311	0912

Note: backstitch lines on wings in dark blue; each antenna is made with one black straight stitch.

PAINTED LADY ▲		ANCHOR	DMC	MADEIRA
·	White	1	White	White
■	Black	403	Black	Black
□	Dark brown	905	3031	2003
V	Light brown	375	420	2104
X	Deep orange	316	740	0204
⋅⋅	Light orange	314	741	0201

Note: backstitch lines on wings in black; each antenna is made with one black straight stitch.

Garden Birds

hese cards, each featuring a
ature study of a favourite garden
tor, may be used to say many
s: the goldfinch for good luck,
ups, or the robin for Christmas
ngs; whatever the occasion, the
ecipient will feel special.

GARDEN BIRDS

YOU WILL NEED

For each card, with a square aperture measuring 6.8cm (2⅝in) each way:

12.5cm (5in) square of cream, 11-count Aida fabric
Stranded embroidery cotton in the colours given in the appropriate panel
No24 tapestry needle
Card, as specified above (for suppliers, see page 40)

NOTE: one skein of each colour on the combined list is sufficient for all five designs. The fabric quantity quoted above includes an allowance of 6.5cm (2½in) each way, for framing; if you are making more than one card, allow a 10cm (4in) square for each, plus a 5cm (2in) margin around the total area.

•

THE EMBROIDERY

Prepare the fabric as described on page 4; find the centre by folding the fabric in half and then in half again, and lightly pressing the folded corner, or by marking the horizontal and vertical centre lines with basting stitches in a light-coloured thread. If you are stitching several designs at once, separate the card areas (10cm/4in square) with lines of basting stitches, and mark the centre of each area, but do not cut them apart until you have finished the embroidery. Mount the prepared fabric in a hoop or frame.

Following the chart, complete all cross stitching, using two strands of thread in the needle. Be careful not to take dark threads across the back of the work in such a way that they show through on the right side. Finish with the backstitching, again using two strands of thread. Stitch each bird's eye, indicated by a black dot on the chart, with a single french knot.

GARDEN BIRDS (all five)		ANCHOR	DMC	MADEIRA
▩	Black	403	Black	Black
·	White	1	White	White
V	Medium grey	399	318	1802
··	Light grey	398	415	1803
I	Light beige	852	3033	2109
+	Yellow beige	373	422	2103
2	Light brown	310	780	2009
⊞	Dark brown	360	898	2005
■	Dark red	20	498	513
□	Red	19	347	510
●	Deep pink	39	309	507
○	Light pink	33	3706	409
H	Deep orange	332	946	0207
↓	Light orange	316	740	204
∷	Yellow green	278	472	1414
◇	Olive	280	733	1611
⊓	Medium green	257	905	1412
X	Dark green	268	937	1504
=	Blue	979	312	1010

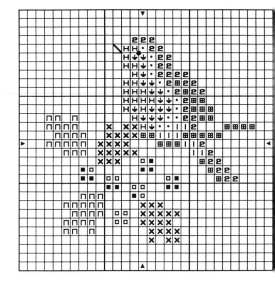

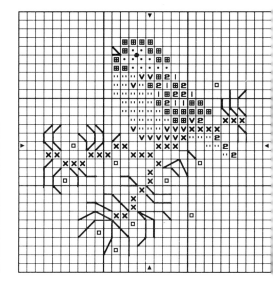

TREE SPARROW ▶		ANCHOR	DMC	MADEIRA
·	White	1	White	White
	Black*	403	Black	Black
⊞	Dark brown	360	898	2005
2	Light brown	310	780	2009
I	Light beige	852	3033	2109
··	Light grey	398	415	1803
V	Medium grey	399	318	1802
X	Dark green	268	937	1504
□	Red	19	347	510

Note: backstitch the fir cone outlines in dark green and the beak in black (used for back-stitching and french knot only); make the eye with one black french knot.*

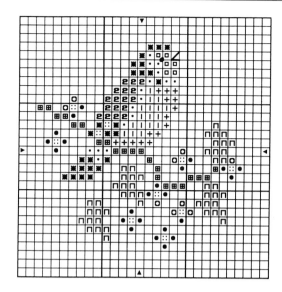

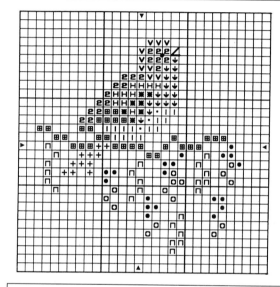

GOLDFINCH ◄

		ANCHOR	DMC	MADEIRA
✳	Black	403	Black	Black
•	White	1	White	White
⊞	Dark brown	360	898	2005
2	Light brown	310	780	2009
I	Light beige	852	3033	2109
+	Yellow beige	373	422	2103
◻	Red	19	347	510
⊓	Medium green	257	905	1412
∷	Yellow green	278	472	1414
●	Deep pink	39	309	507
○	Light pink	33	3706	409

Note: backstitch the beak in black, and make the eye with a black french knot.

ROBIN ◄

		ANCHOR	DMC	MADEIRA
	Black*	403	Black	Black
•	White	1	White	White
I	Light beige	852	3033	2109
2	Light brown	310	780	2009
⊞	Deep brown	360	898	2005
⊓	Medium green	257	905	1412
✕	Dark green	268	937	1504
◻	Red	19	347	510
◼	Dark red	20	498	513
↓	Light orange	316	740	204
H	Deep orange	332	946	0207

Note: backstitch the beak in black (used for backstitching and french knot only), and make the eye with a black french knot.*

BRAMBLING ▲

		ANCHOR	DMC	MADEIRA
•	White	1	White	White
✳	Black	403	Black	Black
⊞	Dark brown	360	898	2005
2	Light brown	310	780	2009
I	Light beige	852	3033	2109
+	Yellow beige	373	422	2103
↓	Light orange	316	740	0204
H	Deep orange	332	946	0207
O	Light pink	33	3706	409
●	Deep pink	39	309	507
V	Medium grey	399	318	1802
⊓	Medium green	257	905	1412

Note: backstitch the beak in black, and make the eye with a black french knot.

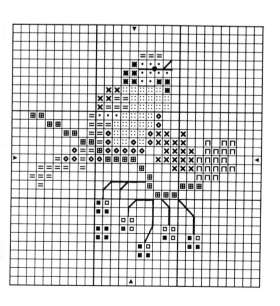

BLUE TIT ◄

		ANCHOR	DMC	MADEIRA	
•	White	1	White	White	*Note: backstitch the*
✳	Black	403	Black	Black	*cherry stems in dark*
=	Blue	979	312	1010	*green, and the head*
⊞	Dark brown	360	898	2005	*and beak in black;*
⊓	Medium green	257	905	1412	*make the eye with a*
✕	Dark green	268	937	1504	*black french knot.*
◻	Red	19	347	510	
◼	Dark red	20	498	513	
∷	Yellow green	278	472	1414	
◇	Olive	280	733	1611	

Butterfly Frames

A set of picture frames with borders of tiny peacock butterflies provides a charming way to display a group of family photographs. The frame sizes can easily be altered by adding or subtracting butterflies, or adjusting the spacing between motifs.

BUTTERFLY FRAMES

YOU WILL NEED

For each large [medium/small] frame, measuring 29.5cm × 25cm (11¾in × 10in) [25cm × 21cm (10in × 8¼in)/21cm (8¼in) square]:

38cm × 33cm (15in × 13in [33cm × 28cm (13in × 11in/28cm (11in) square] of antique white, 14-count Aida fabric
Stranded embroidery cotton in the colours given in panel
No26 tapestry needle
Plain white cotton fabric: one piece 35.5cm × 30.5cm (14in × 12in) [30.5cm × 28cm (12in × 11in/25cm (10in) square], and one piece 29cm × 20cm (11½in × 8in/ [22.5cm × 20cm (9in × 8in/20cm (8in) square]
Medium thickness card: two pieces 29.5cm × 25cm (11¾in × 10in [25cm × 21cm (10in × 8¼in)/21cm (8¼in) square], one of them with a 17.5cm × 12.5cm (7in × 5in) [12.5cm × 8.5cm (5in × 3½in)/8.5cm (3½in square] aperture, and one piece 25cm × 8.5cm (10in × 3½in) [20cm × 8.5cm (8in × 3½in)/17.5cm × 8.5cm (7in × 3½in)]
Synthetic batting/wadding, cut to match the card with an aperture
75cm (29½in) [50cm (20in)/45.5cm (18in)] of thin white cord
Matching sewing cotton
Fabric glue and masking tape

NOTE: for the large and medium frames you will require two skeins of each of the greens.

•

ADJUSTING THE SIZE

The chart shown is for the small square frame; this can be adjusted for the other two sizes simply by adding a butterfly to each side, for the medium frame, and by adding two to each side and one to the top and bottom, for the larger frame. Allow a spacing of two squares between each pair of butterflies; the green border lines are easily extended as the pattern is random, the two tones of green being alternated every few stitches.

THE EMBROIDERY

Prepare the fabric as described on page 4; find the centre by marking the horizontal and vertical centre lines with basting stitches. Mount the fabic in a frame (see page 5) and start the design with the butterflies at the top (middle) of the frame; you will need to count very carefully from the centre point to find the correct position.

Use two strands of thread in the needle throughout. Complete all the cross stitching and finish with the antennae.

MOUNTING AND FRAMING

Remove the finished embroidery from the frame and press lightly on the wrong side, using a steam iron. Spread glue on the side of the mounting card with the aperture, and lightly press the batting to the surface. Place the card, padded side down, on the back of the embroidery, using the basting stitches to check that the embroidery is centred. Fold the fabric over the sides and secure to the card with glue; repeat at the top and bottom. When the glue has dried, cut out the centre, leaving an allowance of about 2.5cm (1in) of fabric for turning. Snip carefully into the corners; fold each of the flaps over the card, and glue (C). When the glue has dried, tape the edges for additional strength. Finally, remove the basting stitches and stitch cord around the frame opening, making a small loop at each corner (D); the ends of the cord start and finish at the back of the mount.

Place the backing card on the larger piece of fabric and secure, making mitred corners (see page 7) and gluing each fold (E). Place the front and back of the frame together, with wrong sides facing (F), and stitch round the sides. Insert your picture and stitch across the opening.

To make the prop, centre the small piece of card over the remaining piece of fabric. Bring the top and bottom edges of the fabric over the card, and tape them in place. Next, bring one side edge over the card and tape that also. Make a 12mm (½in) fold along the free edge, and bring this folded edge over the other, taped side edge. Hem the folded edge in position. Centre the fabric-covered prop at the back of the frame, with the seam facing the mount and the lower edge of the prop level with the base of the frame. Neatly stitch the top edge of the prop to the mount (G).

For the holding cord, using all six strands of stranded cotton, make a knot at the inside back of the prop, about 2.5cm (1in) up from the lower edge, and 6mm (¼in) from the centre; with one long stitch, take the cotton through the fabric at the back of the mount, again about 2.5cm (1in) up from the lower edge, then take it back to the prop on the other side of the centre line. Draw the thread through until the picture stands at the desired angle, then secure the thread with a second knot (H).

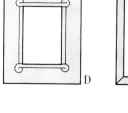

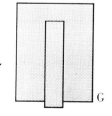

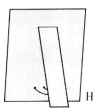

BUTTERFLY FRAMES ▲		ANCHOR	DMC	MADEIRA
○	Light green	244	987	1403
●	Dark green	246	895	1405
∷	Lilac	108	210	0803
▪▪	Blue	118	340	0804
•	Lemon	301	744	0110
◇	Beige	373	3046	2103
+	Salmon	339	920	2009
×	Deep red	20	814	2005
◆	Medium brown	358	433	513
□	Dark brown	905	3031	510
■	Black	403	Black	507

Note: each butterfly antenna is made with one straight stitch in black

Birds of Paradise

This glowing aviary, full of highly-coloured birds, apparently deep in conversation, would look stunning in a kitchen or a child's room. If you don't want to stitch this design as a picture, you might use it for a cushion cover.

BIRDS OF PARADISE

YOU WILL NEED

For the picture, set in a frame with an internal
measurement of 40cm × 30cm (15³⁄₄in × 11³⁄₄in):

*50cm x 46cm (20in × 18in) of white, 14-count Aida
fabric*
*Stranded embroidery cotton in the colours given in
panel*
No24 tapestry needle
Picture frame, as specified above
Firm card to fit the frame
*Lightweight synthetic batting/wadding, the same size
as the card*
Strong thread for mounting
Glue stick
*Coloured card mount to fit the frame, with a cut-out
measuring 33cm × 23cm (13in × 9in)*

●

THE EMBROIDERY

Prepare the fabric as described on page 4; find the
centre either by folding the fabric in half and then
in half again, and lightly pressing the folded corner,
or by marking the horizontal and vertical centre
lines with basting stitches in a light-coloured thread.
Mount the fabric in a frame (see page 5) and start
the design from the centre.

Following the chart, complete all the cross
stitching first, using two strands of thread in the
needle. Finish with the backstitching, again using
two strands of thread. Be careful not to take dark
threads across the back of the work in such a way
that they show through on the right side.

MOUNTING AND FRAMING

Remove the finished embroidery from the frame
and wash if necessary, then press lightly on the
wrong side, using a steam iron. Spread glue evenly
on one side of the mounting card with the aperture,
and lightly press the batting to the surface. Lace
the embroidery over the padded surface (see page
7), using the basting stitches (if any) to check that
the embroidery is centred over the card. Remove
basting stitches; place the mounted embroidery in
the frame, and assemble the frame according to the
manufacturer's instructions.

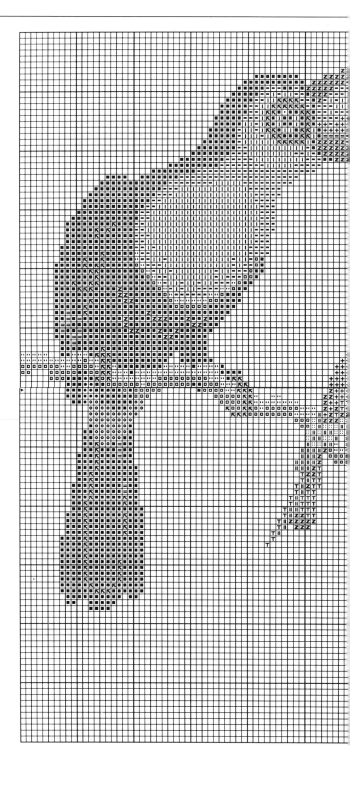

BIRDS OF PARADISE ▲	ANCHOR	DMC	MADEIRA
• White	1	White	White
■ Black	403	Black	Black
◥ Silver grey	399	393	1802
= Dark grey	400	317	1714
∣ Yellow	295	726	0109

		ANCHOR	DMC	MADEIRA			ANCHOR	DMC	MADEIRA
+	Orange	303	742	0114	T	Grass green	257	905	1412
○	Red	335	606	0209	‖	Dark green	246	895	1405
●	Deep red	46	666	0210	⊓	Medium brown	358	433	2008
▬	Yellow green	279	734	1610	☐	Dark brown	360	898	2006
Z	Dark olive	281	732	1613	∷	Medium blue	146	798	1004

Butterfly Babies

Cross-stitched butterflies in delicate blues and greens make a charming addition to baby clothes, whether for a little boy or a girl. Using the waste canvas technique, these small motifs can be stitched to a wide range of purchased garments.

BUTTERFLY BABIES

For each item:

*14-count waste canvas (for suppliers, see page 40) –
a piece approximately 2.5cm (1in) larger all
around than the finished motif(s)
Stranded embroidery cotton in the colours
given in panel
Sharp-pointed needle
Tweezers*

*NOTE: for best results, use garments made of non-
stretch fabrics. If you are not stitching all the designs,
you may not require all the colours listed in the key –
check your chosen chart to see which symbols are
used and which threads you will need.*

•

THE EMBROIDERY

Centre the waste canvas over the area where the motif is to be stitched and pin it in position; use the blue threads in the canvas to ensure that the finished embroidery lies straight on the garment, aligning them either with the weave of the fabric or with the seams of the garment, whichever is appropriate. Start the design from the centre, treating each pair of canvas threads as one. The pins may be removed after a few stitches have secured the canvas to the garment.

Following the chart, cross stitch in the usual manner, using two strands of thread in the sharp-pointed needle; take care to stitch through the holes and not the canvas, as the latter would make it difficult to withdraw the threads. Finish with the backstitching, again using two strands of thread.

•

FINISHING

When you have finished the embroidery, cut away surplus canvas, leaving about 12mm (½in) of waste canvas around the design. Either dampen the right side with slightly warm water and leave it for a few minutes until the sizing in the canvas softens, or hand wash in lukewarm water with a mild soap, rinse in cool water, then roll the garment in a towel to absorb excess water (do not wring it, as this may twist the threads). Gently remove the canvas threads, one at a time, with tweezers. The threads should

come out easily, but the operation requires patience; if you try to remove several threads at once this could spoil your embroidery. Dry and press the garment according to the manufacturer's instructions.

FURTHER IDEAS

These little motifs can be used in many ways. You might, for example, place them one beneath the other down the front of a dressing gown, or use a range of sizes on the same outfit. If you choose, you can easily change the colours to match a particular garment, as long as you have three tones each of two different colours.

As already pointed out, it is not easy to use the waste canvas technique with stretch fabrics; one way to overcome the problem is to iron a small piece of interfacing to the back of the area where you want to stitch your motif, then use waste canvas in the normal way.

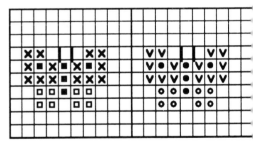

BABYSUIT

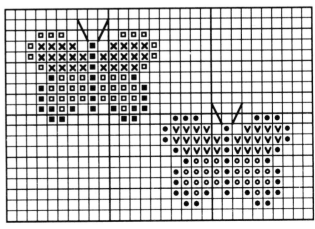

BABYGRO

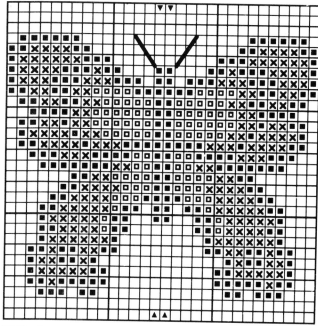

BLUE TOWEL

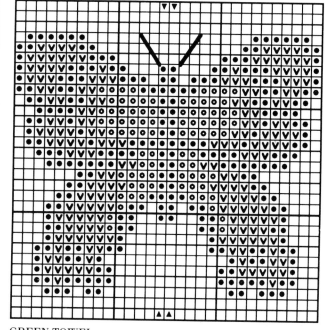

GREEN TOWEL

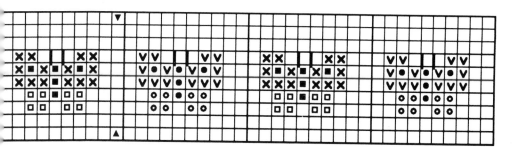

BABYSUIT (SLEEVE)

BUTTERFLY BABIES		ANCHOR	DMC	MADEIRA
■	Medium blue	146	798	1012
□	Light blue	145	799	1013
☒	Pale blue	144	800	1014
●	Medium green	205	912	1213
○	Light green	204	913	1212
V	Pale green	203	563	1211

Note: make the antennae with straight stitches, using medium blue for blue butterflies and medium green for the green ones.

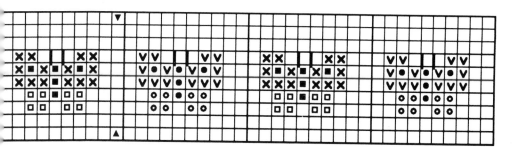

ACKNOWLEDGEMENTS

My grateful thanks go to my family for their invaluable
help. I would like to thank all those who helped to stitch
my projects, in particular Lynn Robinson and my
daughter Elizabeth Marsh.

SUPPLIERS

The baby garments on page 36 were supplied by

Little Treasures
Havant Hypermarket
Purbrook Way
Havant
Hampshire PO9 3QW
Telephone 01705 492339

All fabrics and threads were supplied by Coats Paton Crafts (see below) and the coasters on page 20 were supplied by Framecraft Miniatures Limited, a mail order company that is also a useful source of supply for other cross stitch items, including blank embroidery cards, picture frames and linens:

Framecraft Miniatures Limited
372/376 Summer Lane
Hockley
Birmingham, B19 3QA
England
Telephone: 0121 212 0551

*Addresses for Framecraft
stockists worldwide*
Ireland Needlecraft Pty Ltd
2-4 Keppel Drive
Hallam, Victoria 3803
Australia

Danish Art Needlework
PO Box 442, Lethbridge
Alberta T1J 3Z1
Canada

Sanyei Imports
PO Box 5, Hashima Shi
Gifu 501-62
Japan

The Embroidery Shop
286 Queen Street
Masterton
New Zealand

Anne Brinkley Designs Inc.
246 Walnut Street
Newton
Mass. 02160
USA

S A Threads and Cottons Ltd.
43 Somerset Road
Cape Town
South Africa

For information on your
nearest stockist of
embroidery cotton,
contact the following:

DMC
(also distributors of Zweigart
fabrics)

UK
DMC Creative World Limited
62 Pullman Road, Wigston
Leicester, LE8 2DY
Telephone: 0116 2811040

USA
The DMC Corporation
Port Kearney Bld.
10 South Kearney
N.J. 07032-0650
Telephone: 201 589 0606

AUSTRALIA
DMC Needlecraft Pty
P.O. Box 317
Earlswood 2206
NSW 2204
Telephone: 02599 3088

COATS AND ANCHOR
Coats Paton Crafts
McMullen Road
Darlington
Co. Durham DL1 1YQ
Telephone: 01325 381010

USA
Coats & Clark
P.O. Box 27067
Dept CO1
Greenville
SC 29616
Telephone: 803 234 0103

AUSTRALIA
Coats Patons Crafts
Thistle Street
Launceston
Tasmania 7250
Telephone: 00344 4222

MADEIRA

UK
Madeira Threads (UK) Limited
Thirsk Industrial Park
York Road, Thirsk
N. Yorkshire, YO7 3BX
Telephone: 01845 524880

USA
Madeira Marketing Limited
600 East 9th Street
Michigan City
IN 46360
Telephone: 219 873 1000

AUSTRALIA
Penguin Threads Pty Limited
25-27 Izett Street
Prahran
Victoria 3181
Telephone: 03529 4400